MORGAN COUNTY PUBLIC LIBRARY
110 SOUTH JEFFERSON STREET
MARTINSVILLE, IN   46151

W9-BZA-353

J   Andryszewski,
949.7103   Tricia, 1956-
AND
           Kosovo.

KOSOVO

THE SPLINTERING OF YUGOSLAVIA

Tricia Andryszewski

THE MILLBROOK PRESS
Brookfield, Connecticut

Published by The Millbrook Press, Inc.
2 Old New Milford Road
Brookfield, CT 06804
www.millbrookpress.com

Library of Congress Cataloging-in-Publication Data
Andryszewski, Tricia, 1956–
Kosovo: the splintering of Yugoslavia / Tricia Andryszewski.
p. cm.
Includes bibliographical references and index.
ISBN 0-7613-1750-3 (lib. bdg.)
1. Kosovo (Serbia)—History—Civil War, 1998—Juvenile literature.
2. Yugoslavia—History—Juvenile literature. 3. Yugoslavia—Ethnic
relations—Juvenile literature. I. Title.
DR2087.A53   2000   949.7103—dc21   99-048933

Text copyright © 2000 by Tricia Andryszewski
Printed in the United States of America
All rights reserved
5 4 3 2 1

Cover photographs courtesy of © Art Zamur/Liaison Agency and © Vic
Hinterlang/Impact Visuals

Photographs courtesy of © Niko Economopoulos/Magnum Photos: p. 4;
Sygma: pp. 5 (top © Spencer Platt), 24 (© A. Nogues), 26 (© Tomislav
Peternek), 32 (© Tomislav Peternek), 41 (© Ilkka Uimonen), 51 (©
Tomislav Peternek), 55 (© Patrick Robert); © Havir/SABA: p. 5 (bottom);
Underwood Photo Archives, S.F.: p. 6; Liaison Agency: pp. 10 (© Jean-Luc
Moreau), 16 (© Art Zamur), 29 (© Laurent Van Der Stockt), 36, 48 (©
6492/Gamma), 56 (© Christopher Cox/FSP); © 1999 Owen/Black Star: p.
15; Reuters/Archive Photos: pp. 34 (© Yannis Behrakis), 39 (© Goran
Tomasevic), 43 (© Pawel Kopczynski), 46 (© Emil Vas), 59 (© Nikola
Solic); © Alex Durant/Panos Pictures: p. 31; AP/Wide World Photos: p. 52.
Maps by Michael Mills.

Contents

Refugees

"The police came to my house and told us we had to leave. I asked what do we do, and the police told me and my family to go or be shot.... People are killed. Everything is burned. We have nothing."

"The soldiers told us to leave the village by five o'clock. We have nothing with us, no bread, no water.... They looted the homes and took everything of worth, and after, they burned the village."

"We were scared. They said, 'You have half an hour to get out of here and say hello to President Clinton. You don't belong here. It's not your land, Kosovo.'"

"They gathered us together with the rest of the people from the village. Then, at about seven in the morning, they separated out forty younger males and shot them with machine guns."

"They killed my ten brothers, and I am alone.... On Friday the police came early in the morning—they executed almost one hundred people. They killed them all—men, women, and children. They set a fire and threw the bodies in the fire and put car tires on the fire."

"They rounded up all the villagers. They separated men from women. To the women they said, 'You may go to the border,' and they put us men in two big rooms. They said, 'Now NATO can save you,' and then they started to shoot. And when they finished shooting us they covered us with straw and corn and set it on fire. We were one hundred and twelve people. I survived with one other man."

A family must leave its home and become refugees from the horror of war.

"They kept saying they were going to kill us…. They said: 'Where is your America now? Where is NATO? Why doesn't London or Germany come to protect you?' When we got to the main road they separated some of the men…. The trucks came to take us. As we were getting on they took two people away and killed them. One of them…was a mute and couldn't say anything when they asked him to speak Serbian, so they shot him."

Confusion reigns at a border crossing as a tired boy weeps.

"We left Pec at 11:00 in the morning. At the village of Zrce, the convoy stopped on the main road. There were fifty buses and trucks. It was about 1:30…. There were about a hundred of us on the bus, packed in. There were soldiers on the sides of the road, and armored personnel carriers parked all around as well. Some of the soldiers started pointing at people: 'You, you, and you—get off the bus.' They took them about ten to fifteen meters away, out of sight. We heard shooting. They were all young boys…. When we drove past I saw blood on the road. There were soldiers all around."

"The people leaving in tractors they didn't search so much. The people with good cars, they searched very well. They took the foreign currency, and then they took the cars. They took all our identity documents and burned them, and they took the plates off the cars. Without identity we won't have the right to be back in our own country."

A mother and her children walking toward the border.

"Please help us. You see my baby asleep. I don't know where to go. Not just I, but all the people from Kosovo. Please help us."

Hundreds of thousands of refugees streamed out of Kosovo in early 1999, telling terrible stories such as these. Why was this happening? How did Kosovo become such a killing field?

Chapter 1

Many Peoples, Ancient Conflicts

Kosovo is a tiny land, somewhat smaller than the state of Connecticut, located in a part of the world called the Balkans. "Balkans" means "mountains" in Turkish, and this is a mostly mountainous place in southeastern Europe.

The states of the Balkans include Albania, mainland Greece, Bulgaria, parts of Turkey and Romania, and most of the small states that used to be united as Yugoslavia. The former Yugoslav states include: Slovenia, Croatia, Bosnia, Macedonia, Montenegro, and Serbia, which includes the province of Kosovo.

A tangle of different ethnic, language, and religious groups live intermingled in what used to be Yugoslavia. ("Yugoslavia" means "southern Slavs' land.") Many are Slavic peoples, who speak closely related Slavic languages:

Opposite:
Lake Ochrida, on the border of Yugoslavia and Albania in this extremely mountainous region.

Serbs, Croats, Slovenes, Bosnians, Montenegrins. Macedonians have close ties to both Greek and Slavic culture. Albanians are not Slavs, and their language is not closely related to the Slavic languages.

Three major religions are practiced in the former Yugoslavia. Most Albanians and Bosnians are Muslim. Serbs, Montenegrins, and Macedonians are mostly Eastern Orthodox Christian. Croats and Slovenes are mostly Roman Catholic.

Kosovo is the poorest and most densely populated part of the former Yugoslavia. In 1998, about 90 percent of its 2 million people were Albanians; the rest were mostly Serbs. Albanians in Kosovo then had the highest birthrate in Europe—much higher than Serbs. Between 1961 and 1998 the total number of Albanians in Kosovo nearly tripled, from about 650,000 to about 1,800,000.

Serbs have long complained that as the number of ethnic Albanians in Kosovo has grown, Serbs have been forced out. It is true that, because the Albanian population has grown so fast, the percentage of Serbs in the population of Kosovo has shrunk—from 24 percent in 1961 to about half that in 1981 and only about 10 percent in the 1990s. Nonetheless, the total number of Serbs in Kosovo remained roughly the same (somewhat over 200,000) from 1961 to the 1990s.

Centuries of Conflict

Much of the time, the different peoples of the Balkans have lived together more or less in peace. They've done business together and even married one another. But conflict between various groups has broken out many times as well, over hundreds of years.

That whole story starts some 1,500 years ago, when ethnic Slavs spread out from the Carpathian Mountains to occupy much of central and eastern Europe and the Balkans. Serbian Slavs settled in and near the area known

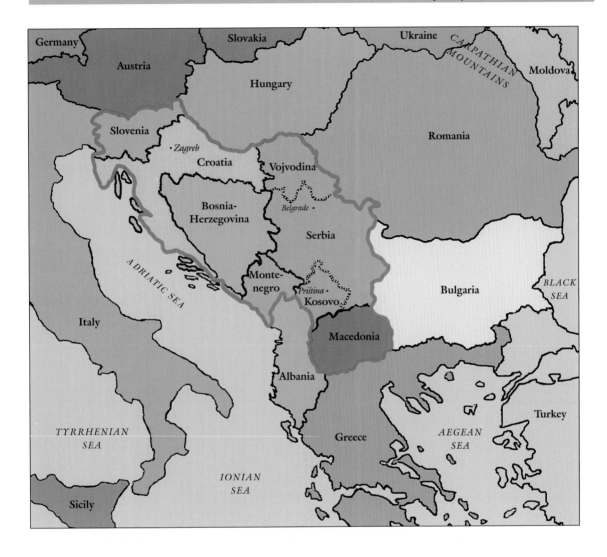

as Kosovo. (Albanians already lived there and nearby. Albanian and Serb historians disagree about just how many Albanians were in Kosovo when the Serbs arrived. Serbs say Kosovo was pretty much empty when they moved in. Albanians say their ancestors were the original natives of Kosovo.)

Beginning about 1,000 years ago, outside forces conquered the various groups of Slavs living in the Balkans. The Serbs came to be dominated by the Greek Byzan-

The republics that were united under Tito into a Communist Yugoslavia.

The Grazanica Monastery, in Kosovo

tines, and most Serbs accepted the Greeks' Orthodox Christianity.

About 1200 A.D., the Serbs overthrew their Greek rulers to form a kingdom centered in Kosovo. Serb farmers and traders clustered in the plains and river valleys of Kosovo. Albanian herders lived in the mountains.

Serbian Orthodox monasteries were built in Kosovo beginning about this time. The monasteries created a rich Serbian spiritual tradition that shaped Serbian identity and nationality. Some of these monasteries are magnificent monuments still standing today.

In the mid-1300s, under their most powerful king, Stefan Dusan, Serbs conquered much of their Balkan neighborhood. Many Serbs feel that the two decades of Dusan's empire were Serbia's glorious golden age. The headquarters for this Serbian empire was the town of Prizren, in southern Kosovo.

Under Serbian rule, Albanians (then mostly Roman Catholic) and other conquered peoples were forced to convert to the Serbian Orthodox church. But not for long. The Serbian empire began to fall apart after Stefan Dusan died, in 1355. Then, during the late 1300s, Ottoman Turks invaded the region. The Serbs' last real stand against the Turks was at the Battle of Kosovo Polje in 1389. Their final and complete defeat by the Turks came in 1459.

The Turks, who were Muslim, stripped Serbian Orthodox monasteries in Kosovo of their riches. Some monasteries were destroyed, and some were turned into Muslim mosques. In the 1600s, most Albanians converted to Islam, while Serbs and many other Slavs remained Orthodox or Roman Christians.

From the beginning of Ottoman Turkish rule in the Balkans, many Serbs, Albanians, and others moved away from their homes, seeking relief from oppression or fighting. Around 1700, this movement of peoples increased. Many Serbs moved northward from Kosovo and Albania, and the center of the Serbs' homeland shifted toward Belgrade. Many Albanians moved into the Serbs' former farmland and villages in Kosovo.

In the 1800s, the Ottoman Empire began to fall apart. In 1878, after years of chaos and fighting, the Serbs overturned Ottoman rule and reclaimed their own kingdom, including Kosovo. Serbs attacked Albanians in Kosovo and tried to drive them out. ("The more Albanians you kick out of our land the greater patriots you will be," the Serbian King, Milan Obrenovic, told his people.) But in the end, other nations in Europe wouldn't allow Serbia to keep Kosovo. Kosovo and most other Albanian-speaking lands remained part of the Ottoman Empire, and still more Serbs left Kosovo and moved north. Albanians, meanwhile, began to demand the right to govern themselves.

World Wars and Communism

Disorder and conflict snowballed in Kosovo at the beginning of the twentieth century. In 1912, Serbia attempted to take Kosovo by force, and Albanians declared an independent state including Kosovo. Various European powers and local ethnic groups fought for control of parts of the Balkans. In 1913, a treaty was signed that carved up the region in a way that made no one happy. Albania lost most of Kosovo to Serbia, and its new borders left more than half of all ethnic Albanians living outside Albania in neighboring countries. Serbia and Montenegro didn't get all of the territory they thought was rightfully theirs, either.

On June 28, 1914, a Bosnian Serb student named Gavrilo Princip assassinated the heir to the Austro-Hungarian throne, Archduke Francis Ferdinand. (Like many Serbian nationalists, Princip wanted to see Serbian territory extended eastward into parts of Bosnia controlled by the Austro-Hungarian Empire.) Austria-Hungary declared war on Serbia. Germany allied with Austria-Hungary. Russia sided with Serbia, followed by Britain, France, and, much later, the United States. The assassination had touched off World War I.

While World War I was an awful war for everyone in the Balkans, Serbs probably suffered the most—as many as one-fifth of all Serbs died. Fighting was especially brutal in Kosovo, with many atrocities committed by Serbs and Albanians against each other.

Peace treaties after World War I drew boundaries for a "Kingdom of Serbs, Croats, and Slovenes," headquar-

What Happened at Kosovo Polje?

Kosovo Polje (Field of Blackbirds), just outside Pristina, in Kosovo, was the scene of a decisive battle between Serbs and invading Ottoman Turks on June 28, 1389. A Serbian prince, Lazar, gathered together an army led by Serbs, Hungarians, Bulgarians, Bosnians, and Albanians to face the Ottoman enemy. "It is better to die in battle," Prince Lazar reportedly said, "than to live in shame." About 30,000 soldiers fought for each side, and most of them died, including Prince Lazar and the commander of the Turkish army, Sultan Murad. At the end of the day, the Turks held the field. But they, too, soon withdrew, so the battle had no clear winner.

The Turks, however, won the war. Too few Serbs were left after this terrible battle to defend their territory, while the Ottoman Empire was able to send in plenty of reinforcements. By the mid-1400s, the Ottoman Turks ruled all of the lands formerly ruled by the Serbs, and most of the rest of the Balkans, too.

tered in Belgrade, dominated by Serbs, and including Kosovo. In 1929, this nation became Yugoslavia. This new nation included several separate republics, rather like the different states of the United States. The Yugoslav republics were: Serbia (including Kosovo), Croatia, Slovenia, Bosnia-Herzegovina (also called Bosnia), Montenegro, and Macedonia.

Albanians were much abused in Kosovo, and in the 1920s some Albanians tried to convince other nations to support giving Kosovo over to Albania. The Yugoslav government encouraged Albanians to leave and Serbs to move to Kosovo, and much Albanian-owned land was seized and given to Serbs. In 1931, fewer than two-thirds of the people of Kosovo were Albanians; the rest were mostly Serbs and their allies the Montenegrins.

While non-Serbian Slavs (Croats, Slovenes, etc.) fared better than the Albanians, they, too, resented Serbian domination through the Yugoslav government. In 1934, the Serbian king, Alexander, was assassinated, likely by Croats seeking independence.

Then came World War II. In April 1941, Nazi Germany, fascist Italy, and their allies invaded Yugoslavia. ("Fascism," like Nazism, means a military-dominated dictatorship with strong economic and social controls and racist characteristics.) The Serbs' King Peter (Alexander's son) left Yugoslavia to be divided among the invaders. Albania was occupied by Italy. Control of Kosovo was split among Germany, Italy, and Bulgaria.

The fascists viewed Slavs (especially Orthodox Slavs) as racially inferior and as enemies, and Serbs and Montenegrins in Kosovo and elsewhere were treated brutally during the war. Albanians fared better, however; most cooperated with the fascists. Croatians were permitted to form their own fascist state. With Italy's support, Croatian fascists forced Serbs living in Croatia to convert to the Croatian branch of Roman Catholicism. Many Serbs who resisted were killed.

Some former citizens of Yugoslavia resisted the fascist occupation. Leading one resistance group, the partisans, was Marshal Tito. Tito won the support of Russia, the United States, and Britain. When these powers defeated Germany and Italy at the end of World War II in Europe, Tito took over as the leader of a reunited Yugoslavia.

Tito was half-Croat, half-Slovene and a dedicated communist. He set up a hard-line communist government independent of the Soviet Union. He also clamped down on ethnic and religious fighting. Yugoslavia's five main Slavic nationalities (Serb, Croat, Slovene, Montenegrin, and Macedonian) each governed its own part of Yugoslavia, minorities were to be respected in all six parts of the country (multi-ethnic Bosnia-Herzegovina was the sixth), and a national Yugoslav government ruled over them all.

For the most part, Tito's ethnic balancing act worked for Yugoslavia—even for minorities living in areas domi-

Marshal Tito is shown here on a hunting trip with the president of Hungary after the two signed a treaty of friendship in 1947.

nated by other ethnic groups. Ethnic conflict was suppressed through the 1950s, 1960s, and 1970s.

Kosovo remained an "autonomous" zone (with very limited self-government) within the Serbian part of Yugoslavia. (The province of Vojvodina, north of Belgrade, also became an autonomous zone within Serbia.) After Tito broke off relations with Soviet Russia and its communist ally Albania, in 1948, Kosovar Albanians were viewed with suspicion by the Yugoslav central government. But persecution of the Albanians was limited. Poverty was a more pressing problem: Kosovo became the most backward, least developed, most over-populated, poorest part of Yugoslavia.

In 1974, a new Yugoslav constitution specifically guaranteed Albanian rights and limited regional self-government in Kosovo. Serbs and Montenegrins resented this special recognition but had to live with it—for the time being.

Chapter 2

Breakup of Yugoslavia

After Tito died in 1980, the old ethnic conflicts slowly rose to the surface again. When communism fell at the end of the 1980s, the many ethnic groups in Yugoslavia's republics once again wanted their own states and would fight to get them.

Milosevic Comes to Power

In April 1987, a little-known politician from Belgrade named Slobodan Milosevic visited Kosovo to attend a Communist Party conference. While he was there, Milosevic gave a rousing speech to a crowd of Serbs about the glories of the Serbian nation. Speechmaking that favored one ethnic group over another had long

Opposite:
In 1988 Slobodan Milosevic, at left, was the leader of the Serbian Party.

been against the rules in Yugoslavia, and when Milosevic broke the rules that day, Serbs in the audience went wild. When some of those Serbs clashed with police, Milosevic told them: "No one will dare to beat you again."

Serbs have a strong emotional attachment to Kosovo. They see it as the home of their greatest kings and, with its many ancient monasteries, the center of the Serbian Orthodox church. When Milosevic spoke out in Kosovo, he became a hero to Serbs throughout Yugoslavia who felt that their interests had been unfairly pushed aside in favor of other Yugoslav ethnic groups. By the end of the year, Milosevic was the most powerful politician in Serbia.

In 1989, Milosevic ended the semi-independent status of Kosovo and Vojvodina and made them completely subject to Serbian rule from Belgrade. Thousands of Albanians were fired from their jobs; many others resigned in protest. Albanians boycotted the new Serb institutions. They instead supported an unofficial government, run by ethnic Albanians, which demanded a return to autonomy for Kosovo.

Milosevic's actions raised uneasy feelings in the other Yugoslav republics: Bosnia, Croatia, Slovenia, Montenegro, and Macedonia. Most of the other republics had more Serbs living in them than Kosovo did. And the other republics certainly didn't want to be ruled by the Serbs in Belgrade.

Meanwhile, between 1989 and 1991, communist governments dominated by Soviet Russia were giving way to local and more democratic rule all over central and eastern Europe. Communism was on its way out in Yugoslavia, too.

Many people thought that the central Yugoslav government should go also, and be replaced by national governments in each of the six republics. The problem with that idea, though, was that each republic had lots of ethnic minorities who didn't want to be ruled (and

Who Is Slobodan Milosevic?

Slobodan Milosevic was born on August 29, 1941, in Pozarevac, a fairly small town in Serbia. His father, a teacher, left the family when Slobodan was still in grade school and returned to Montenegro, where he had been born. His mother was also a teacher, and she was very active in Communist Party politics. Both of his parents ultimately committed suicide, his father when Milosevic was still in college and his mother a decade later.

After earning a law degree at the University of Belgrade in 1964, Milosevic worked for Yugoslavia's communist government in a series of jobs managing economic matters. In 1984 he became a full-time politician when he was elected to lead the Communist Party in Belgrade, the capital of both Yugoslavia and Serbia. In 1987, he rose to power by promoting Serbian nationalism; by 1989 he was president of Serbia.

Milosevic met his future wife, Mirjana Markovic, when they were still in high school. Markovic became a professor of Marxist sociology at the University of Belgrade. She has also been Milosevic's political partner. They have two grown children, a daughter and a son.

A former officer at the U.S. embassy in Belgrade uses the game of chess to describe how Milosevic thinks: "He thinks brilliantly one or two moves ahead, but he doesn't seem to think about the endgame. He's a brilliant tactician, but a terrible strategist. That's why he's led Yugoslavia and Serbia into catastrophe after catastrophe."

maybe abused) by their majority neighbors. For example, Serbs in Croatia feared what a Croatian-run government might do to them without any restraints from a central Yugoslav government. So did Croats and Serbs in Muslim-dominated Bosnia.

In addition, the rest of the world worried that if Yugoslavia broke up, the boundaries between and around the republics might not hold. Might Serbia, for example, try to take over parts of Bosnia where lots of Serbs live? Might Albania or Greece or Bulgaria try to take parts of Macedonia?

Breakup and War

Croatia and Slovenia declared their independence on June 25, 1991. The Yugoslav central government—at this point dominated by Serbs—vowed to stop them, and war began. Within months, Bosnia and Macedonia also broke away from Yugoslavia.

In the fall of 1991, Croatia's government collapsed and Serb forces moved in. Led by Milosevic, Serbs everywhere began to talk of creating a "Greater Serbia," a nation including areas in Croatia, Bosnia, and elsewhere where Serbs were living.

As fighting went on, terrible war crimes were reported. The Serbs made many accusations against Croats and Bosnian Muslims. But most of the war crimes were thought to be committed by Serbs, in areas the Serbs wanted for "Greater Serbia." In a program known as "ethnic cleansing," hundreds of thousands of Muslims and Croats were driven from their homes and tortured, raped, and murdered by Serbs. Bosnians and Croats did also commit war crimes against Serbs.

Most of the fighting took place in Bosnia. One of the hardest-hit areas was Bosnia's capital, Sarajevo, which had long been a multi-ethnic city. In 1992, Serb forces surrounded Sarajevo, cutting off food, supplies, and utilities and bombing residential neighborhoods. Many civilians were killed in the bombing. Others starved and froze during the winter of 1992–1993.

The United Nations began sending food, supplies, and peacekeeping forces to Sarajevo. The North Atlantic Treaty Organization (NATO)—the United States and its Western allies—sent troops to aid U.N. forces.

In January 1994, U.S. President Bill Clinton threatened to use NATO air strikes to stop the Serbian attacks. After a relatively calm summer, fighting broke out again in the fall and continued off and on through the following spring, while peace negotiations muddled along.

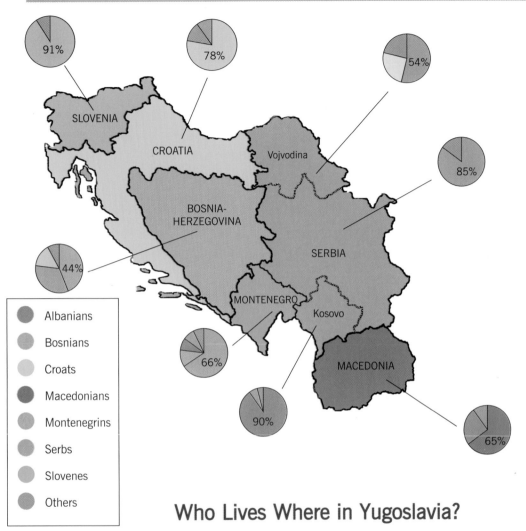

Who Lives Where in Yugoslavia?

Before its breakup in the early 1990s, Yugoslavia included six republics, each with a different ethnic mix:

- Slovenia—more than 90 percent Slovene.
- Croatia—about 75 percent Croat, 12 percent Serb, and much of remainder ethnic German.
- Bosnia—not quite half Bosnian Muslim, about one-third Serb, and the remainder mostly Croat.
- Montenegro—two-thirds Montenegrin, and the remainder a mix of Bosnian Muslims, Serbs, Albanians, and others.
- Macedonia—two-thirds Macedonian, with a fast-growing number of Albanians (one-quarter or more of the population) and smaller numbers of other minorities.
- Serbia—perhaps 85 percent Serb, except for the two semi-independent zones within Serbia: Vojvodina (about half Serb, the remainder mostly Hungarian and Slovak) and Kosovo

In spring 1995, the army of the mostly Muslim Bosnian government launched a major offensive against the Serb forces in Bosnia. Both sides seemed determined to grab as much land as possible before peace was made. The United Nations threatened both sides with air strikes if the fighting did not stop, but the fighting continued and the war planes held their fire.

In May 1995, fighting broke out again in Croatia, which had been relatively calm since early 1992. The Croatian government was trying to regain control of territory seized by Serb forces in 1991; in response, ethnic Serbs living in Croatia fired bombs at the Croatian capital, Zagreb. Some 150,000 Serbs or more were forced to leave their homes in the Krajina region of Croatia. Some of these refugees—Serbian victims of Croatian ethnic cleansing—eventually made their way to Kosovo.

Through June and July, the fighting increased. Serb forces persistently attacked civilian "safe areas" (labeled off-limits for fighting by the United Nations) and gained control of much additional territory. Croats and Muslims escalated their military efforts, too—including attacks on U.N. personnel.

In mid-July 1995, Serb forces took control of Srebrenica, a "safe area" in eastern Bosnia. Tens of thousands of Muslim civilians fled before the Serb takeover. Once in control of Srebrenica, the Serbs began to round up Muslim residents, holding the men (more than 7,000 men were slaughtered) and busing women and children toward territory controlled by Bosnian Muslims.

Soon thereafter, Serb forces took control of Zepa, another "safe area" in Bosnia. At the end of July, two of Bosnia's remaining "safe areas" (Gorazde and Sarajevo) were surrounded by Serb-held territory. Two more (Bihac and Tuzla) were on borders between Serb-held and Muslim-held territory. All of the "safe areas" were surrounded and effectively under siege, with many essential items in short supply.

In late August and early September 1995, NATO aircraft bombed Serb targets in Bosnia for two weeks, while Croatian and Bosnian Muslim forces fought Serb forces on the ground. Ethnic cleansing and related war crimes continued into the fall, even as preparations for peace were under way.

With a sixty-day ceasefire in effect, the presidents of Serbia, Croatia, and Bosnia met on November 1 at Wright-Patterson Air Force Base near Dayton, Ohio, to hammer out a peace settlement. The U.S. government had invited them all there, after getting them to agree in September on some incomplete ideas for peace.

The Dayton Peace Settlement

On November 21, negotiators at Dayton announced that they had reached a peace agreement. (By then, more than a quarter of a million people had died in and around Bosnia and more than two million had been forced from their homes.) After long and thorny discussions, they agreed on exactly how to draw the boundaries within Bosnia between a new Muslim-Croat federation and a new Bosnian Serb republic. Each would elect its own regional president and legislature, and each would retain control of its own taxes, most local matters, and its own army and police. Bosnia's new central government, with a president and a legislature of its own (two-thirds Muslim and Croat, one-third Serbian), would handle foreign affairs and monetary policy for all of Bosnia. Its capital would be Sarajevo. The peace plan specified that 60,000 troops from NATO nations would be sent to Bosnia, beginning in December 1995. The NATO troops would take over from U.N. peacekeepers and maintain the ceasefire, help ensure fair elections for the new governments, and help make other changes outlined in the peace plan. About one-third of these troops were to be U.S. soldiers.

CONFÉRENCE DE PAIX SUR L'EX-YOUGOSLAVIE
PARIS

Seated, from left to right, Serbian President Slobodan Milosevic, Croat President Franjo Tudjman, and Bosnian President Alija Izetbegovic in front of their signed copies of the 1995 Dayton peace agreement, intended to end the vicious fighting that began in Croatia and Bosnia in 1991.

The peace negotiations at Dayton were greatly complicated by the many war crimes committed during the war in Bosnia: the murder and rape of civilians, imprisonment of civilians in concentration camps, ethnic cleansing of entire towns and cities, and other atrocities.

The leader of the Bosnian Serbs, Radovan Karadzic, could not attend the Dayton conference because he was accused of war crimes and wanted for trial by the U.N.–sponsored Yugoslav War Crimes Tribunal. Instead, the Bosnian Serbs were represented by Serbia's President Slobodan Milosevic. Milosevic's hands were not clean, either. His ambitions to build a "Greater Serbia" had been largely responsible for starting the war, and he was generally believed to have encouraged and supported Serbian war crimes. But Milosevic was not actually under indictment for war crimes when the peace talks took place, and peace in the region required his cooperation, so his participation at Dayton was accepted.

The Dayton peace agreement made it illegal for anyone indicted by the U.N.'s war crimes tribunal to hold elected office in any of the three new Bosnian governments. Bosnia, Serbia, and Croatia all agreed to cooperate with the war crimes tribunal, but they did not specifically agree to arrest and hand over for trial any indicted war criminals.

Everyone who signed the Dayton agreement—including Milosevic—also promised to work together to find a peaceful solution to the Serb-Albanian conflict in Kosovo. But no deadlines were set, and no talks were scheduled.

Chapter 3

Toward War in Kosovo

After the Dayton peace accord was signed, several things *didn't* happen in Bosnia:

- Widespread fighting didn't break out again. Local ethnic clashes flared from time to time, but by and large the peace held.

- Most of the refugees didn't return home. With violent Serbian and Croatian nationalists in control of much of Bosnia, hundreds of thousands of refugees were afraid to return to the communities they'd been forced out of by ethnic cleansing during the war.

- Bosnia didn't become a multi-ethnic state. Instead, it split into three zones defined by the ethnic cleansing that went on during the war: 90 percent Croatian in

Opposite: Ibrahim Rugova, voted leader of Kosovo's Albanians in secret elections in 1991-92.

the Croatian zone, 90 percent Serb in the Serbian zone, and 90 percent Bosnian Muslim in the Muslim zone.

- Most of the war criminals were not brought to justice. Although the U.N.–sponsored war crimes tribunal indicted dozens of accused war criminals, hundreds more were not. Of those who were indicted, few were actually caught and put on trial. And the most notorious accused war criminals—Bosnian Serb leader Radovan Karadzic and Serb military commander Ratko Mladic—remained free in the Serb-controlled part of Bosnia and in Serbia.

Changes in Kosovo

While Bosnia was consumed by chaos and slaughter, big changes were under way in Kosovo. In September 1991 and May 1992, Kosovo's Albanians held secret, illegal elections. The voters overwhelmingly favored a return to Kosovo self-government—and they elected a team of leaders to do the job.

The elected head of this new shadow government was Ibrahim Rugova, a Kosovo Albanian professor. Rugova and his followers believed in the power of nonviolence— that a long enough campaign of peaceful resistance (modeled on Martin Luther King Jr.'s campaign in the United States and Mahatma Gandhi's in India) would win the Kosovo Albanians their freedom.

Serbia condemned the secret elections and refused to recognize the results. The Albanians, in turn, refused to recognize the authority of the Serb-run government in Kosovo.

The Albanians began to boycott all Serb-run institutions in Kosovo. And they set up a whole parallel world of their own: Albanian-run schools, hospitals, tax collection, and more.

Kosovo Albanians were bitterly disappointed that the 1995 Dayton peace accord that ended the war in Bosnia did not also force Serbia to restore self-rule to Kosovo. Nonetheless, most Kosovo Albanians remained committed to gaining their freedom through peaceful negotiation. They hoped that finally, with the awful war in Bosnia ended, the world would turn its attention to their cause.

Trouble for Milosevic?

From late November 1996 through January 1997, Serbian opponents of Slobodan Milosevic took to the streets. They were protesting their government's refusal to recognize victories by anti-Milosevic politicians in local elections throughout Serbia. Milosevic's government eventually recognized the new officeholders, but the protests did not lead to Milosevic's fall from power. The anti-Milosevic coalition broke up in the spring of 1997, and in July Milosevic began a new four-year term of office under a new title, president of Yugoslavia. (Yugoslavia was by then made up of just Serbia— including Kosovo and Vojrodina—and Montenegro, which for centuries had been closely allied with Serbia.) In May 1998, Milosevic moved to shut down Yugoslavia's independent TV and radio stations.

By then, however, "separatism" had emerged as a serious threat to Milosevic. Tiny Montenegro seemed headed toward an attempt to break away from Yugoslavia. An anti-Milosevic politician, Milo Djukanovic, was elected prime minister of Montenegro on October 19, 1997. At the end of the following May, Djukanovic's anti-Milosevic allies won big in parliamentary elections.

More dangerous still was the situation in Kosovo— and in neighboring Albania. Communism had ended in

Prime Minister Milo Djukanovic of Montenegro.

Albania in the early 1990s, but no workable system of government or economic management had taken its place. Albania, already the poorest country in Europe, had become even poorer. In 1997, after a government-sponsored get-rich-quick scheme went sour, the government of Albania collapsed. Albanians looted police stations and government armories, and soon Albania was awash in looted guns and ammunition. Many of these weapons were sold and sent across the border into Kosovo.

Toward War in Kosovo

In 1997, a tiny guerrilla force calling itself the Kosovo Liberation Army (KLA) began to wage war against the Serb authorities, mostly by killing Serb policemen. The KLA wanted not just a return to self-government but a total divorce from Serbia, with Kosovo to become part of neighboring Albania.

The on-and-off clashes between Serb authorities and the KLA increased toward the end of 1997 and into 1998. In February and March 1998, the Serbs launched a brutal crackdown in which dozens of ethnic Albanian civilians were killed in a part of Kosovo called Drenica.

The United States and a group of allies (Britain, France, Germany, Italy, and Russia) agreed to impose at least some economic penalties on Milosevic's government if it didn't stop the violence and move toward a peaceful solution to the conflict. On June 12, the allies threatened military action, and on June 16 dozens of NATO jets buzzed near Serbia's borders in a show of force.

The Drenica massacre had big effects inside Kosovo. Up until then, Kosovo Albanians had still generally supported the nonviolent tactics of Ibrahim Rugova. After the Drenica massacre, support shifted to the KLA. The KLA grew, with volunteers, supplies, and money pouring

What Is the
Kosovo Liberation Army?

"When you encounter [the Kosovo Liberation Army]," a human rights observer said in mid-1998, "you may meet a villager with a hunting rifle defending his home, or someone who clearly has had military training—and everything in between."

The Kosovo Liberation Army (KLA) grew from a small band of a few dozen guerrillas in 1997 to a small army of perhaps 6,000 or more by early 1999. This dramatic change happened for several reasons: 1) the vast majority of Kosovo Albanians came to approve of the KLA and offer it support, 2) arms poured in from neighboring Albania, and 3) ethnic Albanians living in the United States and western Europe sent money, communications equipment, and military advisors to help the KLA.

The goals of the KLA were unclear even as it fought an all-out war in Kosovo in early 1999. Everyone involved with the KLA wanted to end the harsh Serb rule over Kosovo. And most wanted to go well beyond the modest goals of Ibrahim Rugova of self-rule for Kosovo within a re-worked version of Yugoslavia.

Many wanted to make Kosovo a part of Albania—maybe even part of a "Greater Albania" covering Albanian-speaking parts of Macedonia and Montenegro, too. And at least some wanted to force all Serbs out of Kosovo—even if they had to carry out their own violent ethnic cleansing to make that happen.

"We really don't know what they are," one European diplomat observed about the KLA in early 1999. "There is an Islamic component, a left-wing [communist] component, and there are those who are just guerrillas."

"Leka," a commander of the Kosovo Liberation Army (UCK in Albanian), at his base.

A demonstration in March 1998 in Kosovo.

in from ethnic Albanians in Albania, northern Europe, and the United States. Soon the KLA became able to wage an ongoing guerrilla war against the much-larger Serbian armed forces.

Fighting between the KLA and Serb forces escalated, threatening to spill over into neighboring Macedonia and especially Albania. American and European diplomats tried to make peace, but neither the KLA nor Milosevic seemed to want a ceasefire. By mid-July, the KLA controlled about one-quarter to one-third of Kosovo's territory. By the end of the summer, perhaps 250,000 civilians had left their homes, fleeing the fighting.

In the fall of 1998, Serbs attacked several ethnic Albanian villages in Kosovo. Dozens of civilians were killed. Threatened once again with NATO air strikes,

Slobodan Milosevic agreed to a ceasefire in October. So did the KLA.

At that point, Serbian military and police controlled the major towns and roads in Kosovo, as well as its borders. The KLA controlled much of the countryside. Some 2,000 unarmed European observers in Kosovo kept an eye on the uneasy truce. Refugees began to return to their homes. The diplomats went back to work on writing a peace agreement.

Then, in January 1999, Serbs massacred forty-five ethnic Albanians in the Kosovo village of Racak. The ceasefire ended.

Some diplomatic arm-twisting came next. Both the Serbs and the Kosovo Albanians were told to make peace or face NATO military action. In February, both sides met for two weeks of talks in Rambouillet, France, with no results. By then, about 2,000 people had died as a result of the fighting in Kosovo over the past year.

After talks began again in March, a peace agreement was written by NATO diplomats. The agreement called for Serbian forces to withdraw from Kosovo and for the KLA to disarm. NATO troops—28,000 of them—would go to Kosovo to keep the peace. The agreement also called for a return to self-rule in Kosovo for the next three years. At the end of those three years, Kosovo might remain part of Serbia or unite with Albania. (The agreement left that question to be decided later.)

KLA and other Kosovo Albanian representatives accepted and signed the Rambouillet peace agreement. Milosevic refused. Instead, he began preparations for a huge Serb military attack on Kosovo.

Chapter 4

Operation Allied Force

On March 19, 1999, the peace talks in Rambouillet, France, between Serbs and Kosovo Albanians broke off. By then, Serbia was moving tanks and tens of thousands of troops toward Kosovo. After the talks broke off, Serb forces inside Kosovo began forcing ethnic Albanians to leave their homes. The United States, Britain, France, Germany, Italy, and Russia kept pressing Serbian leader Slobodan Milosevic to accept the peace deal already signed by the Albanians.

NATO threatened to bomb Serbia if Milosevic continued to refuse to make peace. But U.S. and other NATO officials also insisted that no soldiers on the ground would be sent into Kosovo unless peace was agreed to and both sides—Serbs and Albanians— welcomed the soldiers in to help keep that peace.

Opposite: When they were ordered by the Serbs to leave their homes in early spring, 1999, these villagers piled into their wagons and tractors and headed toward one of Kosovo's borders.

What Is NATO?

NATO (the North Atlantic Treaty Organization) is a military alliance organized after World War II in opposition to Soviet Russia and its allies. NATO is a "mutual defense" alliance; an attack against any one member would be considered an attack against all of them, with all members pledged to fight to defend each other. NATO's members include: the United States, Canada, Great Britain, France, Belgium, the Netherlands, Luxembourg, Iceland, Denmark, Norway, Italy, Portugal, Greece, Turkey, and Germany. In 1998, three former Soviet-bloc nations joined NATO (Poland, the Czech Republic, and Hungary). NATO headquarters is in Brussels, Belgium, but its most powerful member is the United States.

Beginning in March, 1999, NATO bombed Serbia in response to its abuse of Albanians in Kosovo. Russia, NATO's traditional opponent, didn't like this at all. Russians see the Serbs as fellow Slavs sharing closely similar language and religion. In addition, Russia tends to see NATO operations in formerly communist parts of Europe as a threat. (That used to be their turf.)

The obvious alternative to NATO leading military action in Kosovo was for the United Nations to do so. However, international law considers Kosovo to be part of Serbia. Both Russia and China would have vetoed any proposal to have the U.N. send troops to Kosovo against Serbia's will.

The opening session of the NATO summit on April 23, 1999. This summit was intended to celebrate NATO's 50th birthday, but war in Kosovo was the center of attention.

With negotiations at a dead end, NATO told the international observers who'd been monitoring the truce in Kosovo to leave so that they'd be safely outside the country before any bombing started. Once the observers were gone, Serbia began a massive assault on Kosovo's Albanians. The attacks occurred not only in the countryside (where nearly all of the action had happened up until then) but also in the major towns of Kosovo. Thousands of Kosovo's Albanians began fleeing their homes and heading for Kosovo's borders.

Bombing and Refugees

On March 24, NATO airplanes and cruise missiles began bombing military targets in Serbia. For the first few days, the bombing wasn't aimed at Serbian troops and tanks. Instead, the bombers first went after Serbian air defenses and communications equipment, to make the skies safer for the NATO airplanes. The plan was to then bring in a lot more aircraft and hit a lot more targets.

Serbia's response was to step up its military action in Kosovo. With no threat of a NATO ground invasion, Serbia didn't have to concentrate its troops on defending its borders. Instead, Serb forces spread across Kosovo. They went after KLA fighters wherever they could. But most of the action was against Kosovo's Albanian civilians. In a campaign of terror shockingly similar to the "ethnic cleansing" that went on in Bosnia a few years earlier, the Serbs seemed to be trying to force all of the ethnic Albanians in Kosovo out of their homes—and out of the country. "There is a great human tragedy unfolding," one U.S. official said. "Bad stuff is going on, and a lot of it."

Hundreds of thousands of refugees—mostly women, children, and old men—began streaming across Kosovo's borders with Albania, Macedonia, and Montenegro. One after another, the refugees told a horrifying story:

- Serbian army, police, or armed "paramilitary" civilians came to their homes and told them to leave, threatening to kill them if they refused. (Local Serbs identified their homes with marks on the door, so that the ethnic cleansers would pass them by.) As in Bosnia, the paramilitaries included gangs of tough and scary criminals set loose to terrorize the targets of ethnic cleansing.

- Many unarmed Kosovo Albanian civilians were murdered, often in front of members of their families.

- Women were raped, sometimes in public or in front of family members, with the aim of humiliating and terrorizing the Albanian population.

- People who had worked with the international observers and aid workers were especially targeted for violence. So were journalists, teachers, doctors, and other community leaders. Some were tortured before being killed.

- Men of "fighting age" (teenage to about sixty) were separated from their families. There were reports of groups of men being massacred or herded together in stadiums and other concentration areas.

- Whole villages were burned to the ground, apparently to make sure that the refugees who had lived in them would have no place to reclaim.

- On their way to the border, refugees were robbed again and again by armed Serbs.

- Armed Serbs also took away the refugees' identification documents (passports, papers, even car license plates), apparently so the refugees would have no proof that they had ever lived in Kosovo.

Confronted with this huge and growing horror, NATO within days decided to speed up its air campaign and begin targeting Serb troops, mostly by cutting off their

In the city of Pristina, a train packed with people trying to escape Kosovo pulls away toward Macedonia.

supply lines. Meanwhile, NATO losses were minimal. An American stealth fighter jet went down in Serbia on March 27; the pilot was quickly rescued. And on March 31, three U.S. servicemen were captured and beaten by Serbian forces along the Macedonian border. The United States said that they had been taken unlawfully from the Macedonian side of the border and should be freed immediately; Serbia said that they'd been captured inside Kosovo and continued to hold them as prisoners. The three were released in early May.

As the refugees swarmed out of Kosovo in late March, critics of the allied air operation complained that it was failing to stop the ethnic cleansing, and maybe even making it worse—and that NATO military commanders were releasing so little information that it was impossible for the public to know how the war was going. The commanders acknowledged that the bombing campaign had had problems with bad weather. (When it's too foggy or rainy for high-flying pilots to see their targets on the ground, they don't drop their bombs.) NATO also noted that the Serb forces in Kosovo had mostly been working in small groups (hard to see and hit from high in the air) and were being careful to keep tanks and other large pieces of equipment hidden most of the time.

One week after the bombing began, on March 30, NATO officials estimated that more than half a million—about one-third—of all of the ethnic Albanians in Kosovo had been forced from their homes. Long lines of refugees backed up at Kosovo's borders with Albania, Montenegro, and Macedonia.

NATO decided once again to step up its bombing campaign. NATO bombers also began hitting targets in downtown Belgrade. The bombing of Belgrade and other targets in Serbia (police stations, bridges, power plants, gas and oil suppliers) pumped up Milosevic's support among Serbs.

Serb forces began using tanks and mortars to bomb Kosovo villages and towns. They stepped up their ethnic cleansing campaign, emptying out even Pristina, Kosovo's capital city. Here's how one refugee, a woman who fled with her elderly parents, described what happened to her:

> I was watching television . . . and I walked out into the garden and there were three people with black masks and big guns. They wanted to kill my mommy. They said you give me money or I will kill her. I had 550 deutsche marks hidden in my sock and I gave it to him. They were not

policemen. They were criminals Milosevic let out of jail. It is not easy to earn money. But I don't care about the money. They wanted to kill my parents. In every house they broke the doors. When we went out everyone was in the street walking between men with black masks and big weapons. All Pristina is empty today. No Albanians. Only Serbs with guns, they all have guns. Can the world see what they are doing?

Two boys temporarily escape the tedium and stress of life in a refugee camp in Macedonia.

A middle-aged man who left Pristina with his family said:

Four police with masks came in [to our house]. Their first demand was money. The children were frightened and started to cry. We took only the things we had at hand, two blankets for the kids and a plastic sheet in case it rains. All this happened in just five minutes, and we were made to leave our house. On both sides of the street were long lines of Serb police in masks and we had to walk between them to the train station.

On April 2, NATO officials were estimating that half of all the ethnic Albanians in Kosovo had been forced to leave their homes. More than 300,000 had crossed the border since the NATO bombing began on March 24; perhaps 600,000 more were still on the move inside Kosovo.

More than half of those who had left Kosovo were in Albania. Although Albania was the poorest country in Europe and its people had little to share, they welcomed the refugees. Thousands of Albanian families took refugee families into their homes. Still, it was obvious that Albania needed help taking care of so many refugees.

So did Montenegro and Macedonia. Montenegro wasn't a rich nation—and worse yet, it remained part of Yugoslavia. Montenegro had been cooperating with NATO. Its government had stopped taking orders from the Yugoslav government headed by Milosevic. Montenegrins feared that Milosevic (who controlled the Yugoslav army) would try to take over their country.

As for Macedonia, a very young democracy, it had carefully included ethnic Albanians in its government. But the Macedonian majority was uneasy about the rapidly growing Albanian minority concentrated along its border with Kosovo. Macedonians particularly worried

that, if the war ended with Albania gaining all or most of Kosovo, "Greater Albania" might take a large slice of Macedonia as well.

Living conditions where the refugees were massed near the borders of Kosovo were awful; there was little food, shelter, or medical care. On April 4, NATO nations proposed airlifting about 100,000 refugees out of the region and into temporary camps elsewhere. Human rights workers and the refugees themselves protested—

Distress is clearly etched on the faces of these refugees who wait to cross the border into Macedonia.

the refugees wanted to go home, not be scattered far and wide.

Milosevic's "Ceasefire"

On April 6, Milosevic announced a one-sided ceasefire. NATO responded that there was no evidence that the Serbs had in fact ceased firing. NATO said it would continue its bombing until Milosevic agreed to withdraw his forces from Kosovo, to allow the refugees to return home under armed international protection, and to negotiate a political solution to the problem of how Kosovo would be governed in the future.

Overnight, Serbs at Kosovo's borders chased away tens of thousands of refugees waiting in line to get out of the country, forcing the Albanians back into Kosovo. Serbs also began placing land mines along the border. The flow of refugees suddenly stopped. Milosevic proclaimed that the Serbs had defeated the "terrorist" KLA, that negotiations with moderate Kosovo Albanians (including Ibrahim Rugova) were under way, and that there was no reason why the refugees should not feel safe to go home—unless they were afraid of NATO's bombs. (Support for Rugova shriveled when he was shown on television talking with Milosevic.)

When Kosovo's borders were shut down, the United Nations estimated that 303,000 refugees had reached Albania since March 24, and that 117,000 were in Macedonia, and 59,000 were in Montenegro. Many of the refugees in Macedonia had been forced to go to camps away from the border, with many families being broken up in the process.

NATO officials estimated that an additional 300,000 refugees remained trapped in Kosovo. (U.S. officials on April 9 guessed that the number of those trapped in Kosovo was much higher—about 700,000.) No one out-

What Is Genocide?

Slobodan Milosevic and Serbs under his authority have been accused of attempting genocide against Kosovo's Albanians. What does this mean?

After World War II, the United Nations and its member nations decided to make genocide an international crime. In a treaty called the Convention on Prevention and Punishment of the Crime of Genocide, genocide is defined as "any of the following acts committed with intent to destroy, in whole or in part, a national, ethnic, racial or religious group, such as: a) killing members of the group; b) causing serious bodily or mental harm to members of the group; c) deliberately inflicting on the group conditions of life calculated to bring about its physical destruction in whole or in part; d) imposing measures intended to prevent births within the group; e) forcibly transferring children of the group to another group."

side of Kosovo knew where these people were. Perhaps they were hiding in the snowy mountains without food or shelter, perhaps being herded by the Serbs to serve as human shields to fend off more NATO bombing.

And the bombing continued. "This will probably go on for many more weeks," a NATO official said.

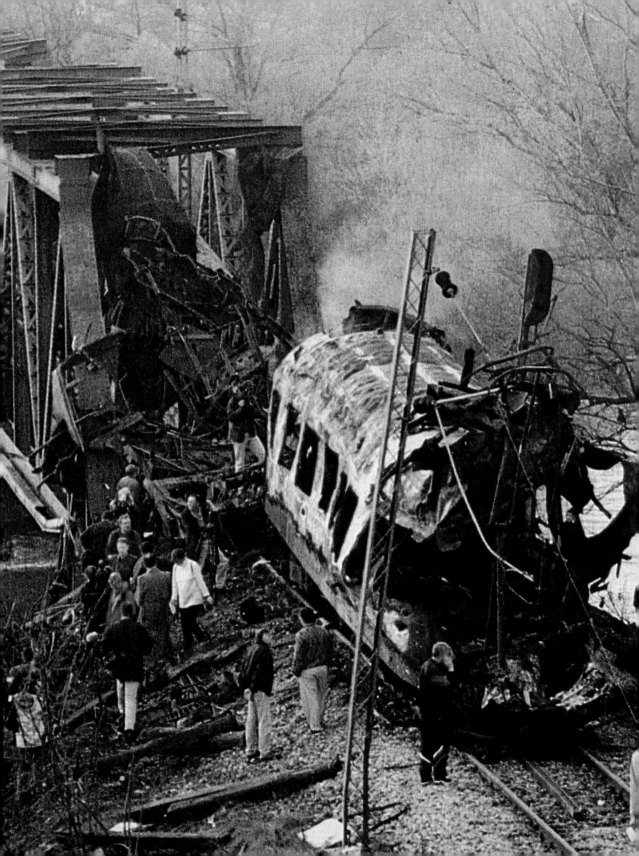

Chapter 5

Endgame

A few days after the Serbs suddenly stopped the refugee flow out of Kosovo, refugees began to trickle across the border again. The NATO bombing continued. On April 12, 1999, a NATO bomber targeting a railroad bridge in southern Serbia hit a passenger train, killing about a dozen civilians. In the following weeks, other NATO bombs went astray and killed Albanian and Serbian civilians.

Through April and into May, Serb forces continued their ethnic cleansing of Kosovo towns and villages. Refugees continued to exit Kosovo; some days just a trickle crossed the border, on other days thousands came. More and more NATO bombs pounded Serbia, often hitting bridges and public utilities, especially the country's power grid. And NATO officials released aerial

Opposite: The wreckage of the bridge and train in southern Serbia.

MASS BURIAL SITE NEAR IZBICA, KOSOVO

NO GRAVES

NEW GRAVES

IZBICA

PRISTINA

NATO photograph showing mass graves. Documentation like this is important in helping The Hague put together a report and bring war criminals to justice.

photos of what seemed to be freshly dug mass graves in Kosovo.

The News From Serbia

Milosevic and Serbia's government-controlled media painted a picture of the war very different from what was broadcast in NATO nations. From the beginning, Milosevic had insisted that Serbian military operations in Kosovo were aimed only at the "terrorist" KLA and that Kosovo's refugees were fleeing NATO bombing, not Serb forces. Then, starting in late April, the Serbian government began saying that the KLA had been mostly defeated and that only NATO's bombing was prolonging the war.

If the bombing would stop, Serbia said, it would welcome the return to Kosovo of the Albanian refugees—but only those who could prove Yugoslav citizenship. Refugees and human rights workers noted that Serb forces had routinely confiscated documents proving citizenship from Kosovo's Albanian refugees. Serbs, on the other hand, claimed that some 300,000 Albanian citizens had illegally moved to Kosovo from Albania in the 1980s.

Serbs may or may not have believed their government's explanation of the war. But while NATO was bombing their country, they overwhelmingly supported their government. "For all his faults, Milosevic is a hero now," said one young man in Belgrade. "The Serbs are proud of fighting for Kosovo, which is ours. We are fighting the greatest power in the world, and even losing proudly is a victory. Just standing up to such power is a victory."

Milosevic on Refugees

"You are right. There are a lot of refugees. But they are a result of [NATO] bombing, and they are not only Albanians. Everybody is running away because of bombing—Serbs, Turks, Gypsy, Muslims. Of course Albanians, their number is biggest. Everybody is running! Deers are running. Birds are running. Everybody is running away because of bombing."

—Slobodan Milosevic, interview for American television, April 21, 1999.

Window of Opportunity

Meanwhile, the press outside Serbia was bitterly observing that bombing alone (without sending in ground troops) had completely failed to prevent or stop ethnic cleansing in Kosovo. Sometime in April, the window closed for sending in ground troops to stop the ethnic cleansing: In the two or three months it would take NATO troops to get there, Serb forces would have plenty of time to completely empty Kosovo of Albanians, if that's what they wanted to do.

NATO's central war goal thus shifted from preventing ethnic cleansing to making it possible for the refugees to return home. And for that, too, a window was about to close. Winter weather sets in as early as October in Kosovo, and the winters there are so harsh that moving troops (let alone refugee families) is difficult and dangerous. It would take months to mobilize NATO troops either to take Kosovo by force or to set up peacekeeping operations in Kosovo and house returning Albanians there before winter. Alternatively, months would be needed to winterize the refugee camps outside Kosovo. NATO would have to choose which course to take soon—by sometime in June.

With that June deadline in mind, in late April and May diplomats stepped up efforts to reach a peace agreement. U.S. and other NATO officials pressed Russia to help find a solution to the crisis that would involve Russian as well as NATO peacekeepers, perhaps under United Nations authority. Russia, which strongly opposed NATO's bombing, became a go-between for Serbia and NATO in talks seeking an end to the war.

These diplomatic efforts were greatly complicated by a terrible NATO bombing mistake. On May 7, a NATO bomb hit the Chinese embassy in Belgrade, killing three and wounding nearly two dozen. China reacted furiously, and hinted that it might block United Nations approval of armed peacekeepers.

Divisions began to open up among the NATO nations concerning the use of ground troops. Great Britain leaned toward sending in troops to take Kosovo by force, if necessary, before winter. Germany strongly opposed this. In late May, after U.S. urging, NATO approved moving 50,000 armed "peacekeeping" troops into place near Kosovo's borders. Whether these troops would be used to implement a peace agreement, invade Kosovo, or help winterize the refugee camps remained undecided.

Under cover of darkness, a NATO bomb finds its target. This television and radio broadcasting building crumbled seconds after this photograph was taken.

Упозорење снагама ВЈ:
НАПУСТИТЕ КОСОВО

НАТО сад употребљава Б-52 бомбардере за бацање МК-82, 225кг. бомби на јединице ВЈ на Косову и Метохији. Сваки Б-52 може да носи више од

50 оваквих бомби!

Ови авиони ће се враћати по вас све док не истерају ашу јединицу са Косова и Метохије и спрече вас у вршењу зверстава. Ако хоћете да преживите да опет видите своју фамилију, оставите своју јединицу и бојно средство

04-NN-17-L002

и одмах напустите Косово и Метохију!

A leaflet printed in Serbian and dropped by NATO into Kosovo. It reads, "A warning to the Yugoslav army troops: LEAVE KOSOVO! NATO is using B-52 bombers to drop MK-82, 225-kilo heavy bombs on your units in Kosovo. Every B-52 can carry more than 50 of these bombs! These planes will keep coming back for you until they expel your unit from Kosovo and prevent you from committing atrocities. If you want to survive and see your families again, leave Kosovo and the battlefield."

Then, on May 27, the United Nations war crimes tribunal issued a warrant for the arrest of Slobodan Milosevic and four other top Serbian leaders, demanding that they be brought to trial for war crimes in Kosovo. Milosevic himself was charged with personal responsibility for forcing some 740,000 ethnic Albanians to leave Kosovo and for the murder of more than 340 identified Albanians in seven specific incidents. Additional counts would likely be added, the tribunal said, as more evidence was uncovered.

Milosevic had additional bad news—from Kosovo. Far from being wiped out by Serb forces, the KLA had grown in strength and effectiveness. By late May, KLA forces in Kosovo numbered perhaps 20,000, with thousands more being trained in Albania. The KLA were mostly farmers, teachers, and tradesmen with little military experience, and they were much less heavily armed than Serb forces. But the Serbs, hounded by NATO bombers, were dug into defensive positions vulnerable to attack by the much more mobile KLA. When KLA attacks drew the Serbs out in the open or simply forced them to reveal their positions by firing back, NATO bombers hit the Serb troops from the air.

Peace Agreement

On June 3, Serbia agreed to peace conditions presented to it by NATO and Russia:

- Serb forces would quickly withdraw from Kosovo.
- All refugees would be allowed to return home.
- Armed peacekeepers, authorized by the United Nations, would occupy Kosovo and protect all of its citizens. The peacekeepers would be under one command, with 50,000 NATO troops (including 7,000 Americans) playing the dominant role.
- The United Nations would help create a temporary government for Kosovo.
- Kosovo would remain part of Yugoslavia but would be permitted to govern itself free of interference from Serbia.
- The KLA would "demilitarize."
- A small number of Yugoslav troops would later be permitted to guard border areas and Serbian Orthodox holy places.

Russia—Serbia's most powerful friend—played a crucial role in persuading Serbia to make peace, and would be key to carrying out the peace agreement. NATO-Russian peacekeeping cooperation got off to a bumpy start when Russian troops moved into Kosovo and occupied Pristina's airport ahead of NATO peacekeepers. Before the end of June, however, Russia and NATO had agreed on how to coordinate their operations. The peacekeeping force, known as KFOR, would include troops of many nations: NATO nations, Russia, and others. Each nation's troops would answer to its own officers, but a unified command (NATO in consultation with Russian representatives) would oversee the whole operation.

Putting the Agreement Into Action

By the time peace was agreed to, more than 900,000 refugees had left Kosovo, most of them during March, April, and May 1999. About 500,000 additional refugees were hiding inside Kosovo, forced from their homes and with little to eat.

For several days after Serbia accepted the peace agreement, Serbian and NATO military officers worked out a detailed plan of action. Serb forces began to withdraw from Kosovo into Serbia, and on June 10 NATO stopped the bombing. The bombing campaign had lasted seventy-eight days.

Almost as soon as the bombing stopped, refugees began to head home, braving land mines, lack of food and shelter, and an uncertain future. "It's better in a tent in my garden than here [in a refugee camp]," said one man whose house had been completely destroyed by Serbs.

As the refugees returned home, tens of thousands of Serb civilians who feared revenge attacks followed Serb troops out of Kosovo and into Serbia. KFOR peacekeepers scrambled to provide security for Serbs and Albanians alike, and to clear roads of land mines left behind by Serb forces. Aid workers scrambled to send in food. (Fighting had prevented Kosovo's farmers from planting crops in 1998 and 1999, and Serb forces had confiscated food and killed livestock. The refugees would be nearly totally dependent on food aid from abroad until well into 2000.)

The returning refugees were met by the KLA. In many places, the KLA organized makeshift local government and worked to restore such basic services as water

French troops are welcomed into Kosovo on June 12, 1999.

supply and electricity. There were surprisingly few reports of KLA violence against Serbs after the peace agreement took effect, and KLA leaders publicly discouraged revenge attacks against Serbs. (There were nonetheless countless reports of looting and destruction of Serb-owned property by Albanian civilians—and dozens of Serbs were murdered or died in fights with Albanian neighbors or KFOR peacekeepers.) For the most part, KLA soldiers cooperated with KFOR. Many handed over their weapons—but nonetheless expected to play important roles in the new, U.N.-sponsored government of Kosovo.

These ethnic Albanian women are looting a Serbian home after the Serbs themselves became refugees as a flood of Kosovar Albanians returned to Kosovo.

For the time being, Kosovo's government would be run by KFOR, with Kosovo divided into five military sectors: French, Italian, German, British, and American. (KFOR troops in all sectors would be multinational. Russian troops would operate in the American, German, and French sectors and at Pristina airport.) In the longer run, though, Kosovo would have a democratic government separate from Serbia, whether or not Kosovo remained officially part of Yugoslavia. Both KLA officers and Kosovo Albanian civilians had in the past decade gained a lot of experience with creating and running their own "shadow" government and other institutions. KFOR and other peace workers made well-publicized efforts early on to find this local talent and put it to work.

Rebuilding After War

There was certainly a lot of work to be done. Food, medical supplies, fuel, and shelter were all in short supply throughout Kosovo. Supply lines would have to be set up before winter. War wounds required medical treatment.

Hundreds of thousands of homes, as well as roads, bridges, and public buildings damaged or destroyed by Serb ethnic cleansing or NATO bombing, needed to be repaired or replaced. Families that had lost all their belongings to fire and looting needed clothing, furniture, and cooking utensils. Farmers needed new supplies and equipment to get to work on sowing winter wheat before the planting season ended. Land mines and unexploded ammunition had to be found and made harmless.

Equally urgently, before cleanup and rebuilding wiped it away, evidence of war crimes had to be documented so that justice could be done. Human rights workers and crime-scene experts from around the world interviewed witnesses, photographed hundreds of crime scenes, and gathered evidence to be later used in trials. What they found confirmed refugees' earlier reports of mass murder and other atrocities. Investigators estimated that at least 10,000 ethnic Albanians had been killed by Serbs during their ethnic cleansing of Kosovo.

Repairing damage from the war would take many years and billions of dollars, mostly from western Europe. Most of this money at first would be humanitarian aid— food, medical supplies, emergency housing. But in later years more and more would be development aid—money for building roads and other infrastructure, for starting or restarting businesses, and for encouraging trade.

The United States, its NATO allies, and Russia all agreed that development aid was needed throughout the Balkans, in Bulgaria and Romania as well as in Kosovo and all the other parts of what used to be Yugoslavia. Unless the whole Balkans region grew economically stronger, better connected with Europe's wealthier economies, and politically more stable, all of Europe's peace and stability would continue to be threatened and more wars would be likely in the future.

However, right in the heart of the Balkans is Serbia. Traditionally the dominant player in Balkan economic

War Crimes Evidence

As Serb forces withdrew from Kosovo, human rights workers moved in to find and record evidence of war crimes. Here are excerpts from a report on evidence of one mass killing:

Accompanied by a local villager, a Human Rights Watch researcher [on June 18] inspected the site of a mass killing in Meja, northwest of Djakovica....

The bodies were found on the edge of a field next to the road that runs through the village of Meja. One intact body and the top half of another body were located on the side of a ravine adjacent to the field, roughly thirty meters up from the road. Another two bodies were a few meters further up the ravine, and the bottom half of another body was located in the field near the ravine. All of the bodies were in an advanced state of decay. The bones of some of the bodies were broken, and they all appeared to be headless. Pieces of a skull were found next to one of the bodies.

Closer to the road, the researcher saw three large piles of straw and cow manure, which the villager said covered many more bodies. The villager also stated that the bodies of most of the men killed in the massacre had been collected by Roma (Gypsy) street cleaners. Having seen the bodies after the massacre, the villager estimated that they numbered well over 100.

In the field were clusters of burned documents and personal possessions—items such as cigarette cases, keys, and family photos—that apparently belonged to the dead men. Spent bullet casings were also littered about....

After nineteen separate interviews with eyewitnesses who had passed through Meja on April 27, Human Rights Watch concluded that at least one hundred, and perhaps many more, men between the ages of sixteen and sixty were taken out of a convoy of refugees by Serbian forces and systematically executed in Meja on that day.

life, Serbia sits astride rail routes, waterways, and roads used for commerce among the other states in the region. NATO bombing did billions of dollars of damage to Serbia—on top of the economic damage inflicted by trade sanctions since war began in Bosnia in 1992. So long as Slobodan Milosevic and other accused war criminals remained in power, western Europe and the United States would continue to shun Serbia, and Serbia's damaged economy could hold back the development of the entire region.

The fate of Kosovo—and of the rest of the Balkans— thus remained tied to Slobodan Milosevic. At war's end, his popularity among Serbia's people was reduced, but for the moment at least his grip on power still held.

Louise Arbour, chief prosecutor of the U.N. War Crimes Tribunal, visits a mass gravesite with British investigators.

Chronology

ca. 500	Slavs migrate throughout central and eastern Europe and begin to settle in the Balkans.
700–900	Outsiders dominate the Slavs in the region that eventually becomes Yugoslavia and convert them to Christianity.
Late 1300s	Ottoman Turks invade south-central Europe and establish Muslim religion and culture.
1389	Turks defeat Serbs at the Battle of Kosovo Polje.
1878	Serbs overthrow the Turks and claim their own kingdom. Albanians begin to demand independence.
June 1914	Austro-Hungarian Archduke Francis Ferdinand is assassinated by a Serbian nationalist, touching off World War I.
1918	World War I ends. The Kingdom of the Serbs, Croats, and Slovenes (later Yugoslavia) is created, ruled by a Serbian king, Alexander.
1934	King Alexander of Serbia is assassinated. Rebellious Croats are blamed.
1939–1945	World War II. During the war, much of Kosovo becomes part of Albania under the rule of fascist Italy.
1945	After World War II, Marshal Tito becomes the leader of Yugoslavia (once again including Kosovo) and suppresses ethnic and religious conflict.
1948	Tito breaks with the Soviet Union and charts a course for Yugoslavia as an independent communist state.
1974	A new Yugoslav constitution guarantees Albanian rights and limited regional self-government in Kosovo.
May 1980	Tito dies.
1980s	Old ethnic conflicts re-emerge as communism crumbles in Yugoslavia.
1987	Serbian politician Slobodan Milosevic visits Kosovo and stirs up Serbian resentment of Albanians.
1989	Milosevic replaces the regional self-government in Kosovo with a hard-line Serb regime. Kosovo Albanians boycott the new Serb government.
1989–1991	Communism ends in the Soviet Union, in the states it dominated in eastern Europe, and in independently communist Albania and Yugoslavia.
1991	Slovenia and Croatia declare independence from Yugoslavia, followed by Macedonia and Bosnia; Yugoslavia's Serb-dominated federal troops begin fighting the Croats; the Croatian government collapses and Serbs take control of much of Croatia. In Kosovo, ethnic Albanians begin to set up a separate government and other institutions.

1991–1995	War among Serbia, Croatia, and Bosnia.	**Fall 1998**	Serbs launch more attacks in Kosovo; NATO threatens air strikes; Milosevic and the KLA agree to a cease-fire.
November 1995	U.S. negotiators and the presidents of Bosnia, Serbia, and Croatia meet in Dayton, Ohio, and reach a peace agreement.	**January 1999**	Serbs massacre forty-five ethnic Albanians in Racak, Kosovo.
July 1997	Slobodan Milosevic is sworn in for four more years in power, now under the title of president of Yugoslavia.	**March 1999**	Kosovo Albanian representatives sign a peace agreement in Rambouillet, France. Milosevic refuses, and Serb forces prepare for a large military offensive in Kosovo.
October 1997	An opponent of Milosevic, Milo Djukanovic, is elected prime minister of Montenegro.		
Late 1997	Clashes between Serb authorities and the Kosovo Liberation Army (KLA) increase in Kosovo.	**March 24, 1999**	NATO forces begin to bomb targets in Yugoslavia.
Early 1998	Serb authorities launch a brutal crackdown in the Drenica region of Kosovo. Dozens of ethnic Albanian civilians are killed.	**March–May 1999**	Serbs undertake massive ethnic cleansing in Kosovo. Hundreds of thousands of Kosovo Albanians flee the country. NATO continues to bomb Serb targets.
May 1998	Milosevic moves to shut down Yugoslavia's independent TV and radio stations.	**May 27, 1999**	U.N. war crimes tribunal issues arrest warrant for Slobodan Milosevic and other top Serb leaders.
June 1998	Serbia is threatened with U.S./NATO action for its military offensive in Kosovo. Dozens of NATO jets buzz near Serbia's borders in a show of force.	**June 3, 1999**	Serbia accepts peace agreement presented by NATO and Russia.
July 1998	The KLA controls perhaps one-third of Kosovo's territory.	**June 10, 1999**	NATO bombing of Serbia ceases. Refugees begin returning to Kosovo.

For Further Reading

Books

Grant, James P. *I Dream of Peace: Images of War by Children of Former Yugoslavia*. New York: United Nations Publications, 1994.

Mead, Alice. *Adem's Cross*. New York: Farrar Straus & Giroux, 1996.

Web sites

www.cnn.com/SPECIALS/1998/10/kosovo Cable News Network's coverage of the war in Kosovo, with background and links to other Web sites.

www.pbs.org/newshour Search here for PBS's extensive *NewsHour* coverage of the war in Kosovo, especially rich in background and first-person interviews.

www.usia.gov/regional/eur/balkans/kosovo Official U.S. government coverage, from the U.S. Information Agency, including information from the United Nations' refugee agency and links to other Web sites.

Index